Slow Kill: Poems

poems by

Jordan Charlton

Finishing Line Press
Georgetown, Kentucky

Slow Kill: Poems

Copyright © 2024 by Jordan Charlton
ISBN 979-8-88838-788-7 First Edition
All rights reserved under International and Pan-American Copyright Conventions. No part of this book may be reproduced in any manner whatsoever without written permission from the publisher, except in the case of brief quotations embodied in critical articles and reviews.

ACKNOWLEDGMENTS

"That's Not Who I Am," "I'm Thinking of a Distant Future," and "I Think I'm Becoming A Regular To This Neighborhood." *Tuskegee Review*.

"Sometimes I Worry," and "It Just So Happens that Today," and "Last Night, While Perched in an Old Oak." *Platform Review*.

"I Tell You the Past is Somewhere We Look When Imagining Costs Too Much." *Rappahannock Review*.

"It Seems in America, Loving Yourself Means Forgetting History" and "Confession." *West Trade Review*.

"Letter to My Unborn Child." *Ruminate*.

"I Would Write But." *Atticus Review*.

"Where There Is No Law." *Brushfire Literature & Arts Journal*.

"Self-Portrait as Unnoticed Object." *Lucky Jefferson*.

"On Darkness". *Typehouse Literacy Magazine*.

Publisher: Leah Huete de Maines
Editor: Christen Kincaid
Cover Art and Design: Isaiah Jones
Author Photo:

Order online: www.finishinglinepress.com
also available on amazon.com

Author inquiries and mail orders:
Finishing Line Press
PO Box 1626
Georgetown, Kentucky 40324
USA

Contents

Dear Reader, | 1

Confession | 3
I Would Write But | 5
I'm About at My Limit | 7
It Seems in America, Loving Yourself Means Forgetting History | 8
I Tell You The Past is Somewhere We Look When Imagining Costs Too Much | 9
America's Dream | 10
Dinner in Sarasota | 13
The Sky is Mute Gray | 14

I Would Write But | 16
There are Times When | 17
America is in An Arms Race with Itself | 19
I Think My Mother Has an Obsession with Our Last Name | 20
I Can't Focus Right Now, Please Call Again | 22
On Darkness | 23
I've Known Memory as a Portal and a Tether | 24
Epistle for My Unborn Child | 25

Slow Kill | 26

I Wait for a Love My Heart Needs | 30
In The Dream I Wake From | 31
Last Night, While Perched in an Old Oak, A Dream | 33
Summer Days Like Today | 34
I Keep Forming Arguments, Sometimes with Myself | 35
Hear Me Out | 36
It Just So Happens That Today | 37
The Darkest Place Under the Moon is Furthest from My Mother's Love | 38
It Just So Happens that Today | 39

On the Occasion I Spent Eight Hours In the Emergency Room | 40
Monet's "Waterlilies" | 41
It Just So Happens that Today | 42
Sometimes I Worry | 43
Making Sense of this New Normal | 44
I think I'm Becoming a Regular to this Neighborhood | 45
I'm Thinking of a Distant Future | 46
8:46 | 47

Where There Is No Law | 49
That's Not Who I Am | 50

Intro | 51

Notes & Additional Acknowledgments | 53

for my mom

Dear Reader,

        I write now thinking much smaller   forgive me   later
I write about

        a boy   &   his mother & love   &   a love that
God   is
black

& I am   right now   interested in   theory about blackness   & masculinity

which   for me sounds   like the footsteps outside of the corner store—
The Temptations or Al Green playing through the stereo
the ways we know it is time for cleaning   to be clean

I am   writing about   our physical health   the quiet nature of dealing with
 disease the quiet nature of the disease of perseverance   about the
health of our families &   about romantic love   &   the butterflies

      & about   what we do with absent   fathers
      & the thin veil of silence we wrap our whole bodies with

for me   all   love   is   about the places I got stuck

                        or just places where I needed more
I have marked
these places in my heart &
have questions
confusion

                      something quiet reminding me of
                      all the poetry I am trying to write

whispers harsh and violent

here is a cliché   these are poems so close to the heart you may
hear them beating
too often
                I bend meaning positioning certain qualities
                      &   when I do that—this kind of move
    I am not quite sure what to call it   &

        I am afraid

&   about the last poem   I have so many feelings   mostly
love for you & for how we find ourselves

with opportunity   I'm tearing up a little I did not think
it was going to circle back to the figure of the mother
I was like no no this is not the right ending

I feel differently because there she is at the end

I am interested to see what   you were thinking   okay that is all for now

thank you again

love —

Confession

I am not a martyr or hero   either
only   a combination   of the rarest qualities

I know   in this life—   black & still alive. I write
still as   a qualifier,   as a condition,   aware

the air could be choked   from this, my one body.
I mean to write   I am black,   which is to say

beautiful, alive,   which is to mean celebrated
with no need for mourning.   I write fearing

I might not live twenty-five   &   my friends
might not either. I can only   register this

with the narrative this country owes
to white supremacy.   I will   not

blame this   on any singular man,
woman, white/black body.   I point

with my arm outstretched   to the root of my terror:
America,   knowing, yes,   my own benefit

from liberties   proposed in writing—
in assembly   or   speech   or   due process,

however,   I know those words were written
for no one who looks like me   or   with skin

like mine—that my blood   might have run
wide as the West   conquered by Destiny,

conquered by God, for He so loved the white man,
He was   made in their image.

I write searching for language
hoping   to recoil the history impressed on me

& that lives   within me, my friends,
with you.

Yes, power needs the oppressed,
wanting what   you can not have freely

for yourself.   For Mr. Floyd, it was air
& for me,   and often for others

this very moment   or
in any   it is   life.

I Would Write But

I can not make a beautiful thing out of my sadness,
so I won't. There is no metaphor for it. I write to say

I have lost hours to tears, lost satisfaction
to hunger—that losing all feels like betrayal,

that my grief takes so much from me, leaves me
consumed in guilt, as if my neat and orderly pain

is less important. But less than what, exactly?
I write thinking if it were nameable, it could not eat me,

thinking the thing eating at my insides
is what might swallow me on the outside.

Call it America, call it an officer of the law.
Call me when the nightmares subside or

when I can sleep through the night again.
I count these weighty moments like so:

sleep feels like nothing. I wake in a new
darkness. When the light of the sun finds me,

we are like unruly children, disturbed.
The afternoon comes with more hunger.

I often fail at feeding myself and yet
still do enough to keep myself alive, keep

this pain living. Have I mentioned the internet?
That's another pain—ephemeral, ghostly,

like any quality haunting is. I wake to the grief—
share condolences to the brothers and sisters

lost to the violences, share condolences
with myself for those I thought were friends

now lost to their silence, knowing empathy
is a work of the imagination, knowing

they have held from me their thoughts, which
I have too many. The worst is the knowing,

knowing this has all been for them & most things
would apply. Life? Yes. Liberty?
Yes. The pursuit of happiness? Yes.

I'm About at My Limit

A notification tells me my screen time is at an all-time high.
I want to tell my phone, I keep trying to escape,
keep trying to look out for something new and interesting, keep
looking because there is no such thing that I have found.
Instead, I exhale a prayer that the newsreel will cease to exist.
I breathe storing in my body a lifetime of joys and new grief.
I close my eyes to the images I wish to share with no one,
instead, in this silence that fills the day perpetually, I miss
the deep bellied laughs of my friends, and waste away
in the difficulty of writing, of trying to make something new.

Everything I love feels old, some unbridgeable distance
from this wandering. Pen in hand, I approach the page with a fear
creeping between stomach and ribcage, insecure that the thing I do
lacks meaning. That it will not be spectacular for you. And that is true.
Today, it will not be dazzling. Today, I want to create spaces
for the one's I love where our shadows can come alive together again.

It Seems in America, Loving Yourself Means Forgetting History

But I won't mention this   in conversation.

It is like, how some experience   time seems

imaginary, like   the plot of folk tales,

urban legends, creation   stories we—

and when I say we, I mean they—

might make up a new ending to, like something

that has been crafted to fit the science   fiction

running throughout our nation & our classrooms.

I write now, remembering, again, that clerk calling us out,

my friend and I, us both like beanstalks,   thin,

and naïve to his attention, asking   no

demanding we empty our pockets or else

we could not leave his store.
                                                                    I mean

to write we were children, & thank our mothers
                                                              we survived.

I Tell You The Past is Somewhere We Look When Imagining Costs Too Much

Please don't ignore me—
        I'm not where I want to be,
                although I don't know where that is

yet. This city and its cottonwood trees
        has become some strange home for me
                I'm afraid I might never escape.

If I planted a seed in the earth,
        I would bring to you the first fruits,
                my soil-stained hands smelling

like labor and desire, what every living creature
        reeks of at least once before dying.
                At least once before dying,

I hope to know that my worry can be curtailed.
        Maybe with a language written outstretched
                by a finger, like a toddler's painting, or

something smaller like the pit in the middle
        of a peach, the core of an apple hidden
                beneath its flesh.

This past summer, I died in the end of most of my dreams.
        I'd wake to the silence of absence, of restless night.
                They are not the same, but they'd feel similar.

No one to tell. No one to wake with me,
        in this city. No one who held me in the quiet sweat
                my fear draped over me.

America's Dream

On a trip back home to visit my mother
she asks that we drive up town for ice cream.

When we get to the multipurpose shopping center
I'm confused. While looking for a parking spot

I mumble what are all these white people doing
here not realizing its loud enough for her ears.

She pleads forgiveness though she is alone
in the car with me. I drive her silver Mercedes

gingerly over the gravel parking lot. Her nerves
won't allow me to forget the tires are aged,

are wearing from the distance passed.
While eating cake batter ice cream,

my question turns in my stomach. She says
this place is so nice; they've made wonderful

strides with this old prison. Prison?
The word becomes sour on my tongue;

makes bitter the cup full of sweet.
We sit on old whiskey barrels, surely

with their own history. The rich brown
spirit the South has nursed its love affairs

with—among them dope, among them fields,
among them people; the peddlers, the workers,

the imprisoned. As cotton-white faces pass
and spend their money wantonly,

I think of the structure of this unholy space,
imagining who might've walked these halls

as ghosts in a time before. Surely, these walls
could tell stories if you pressed hard enough.

If leaned into, what might they say?
What would they confess? I imagine

if they could, they might implicate this rotunda
of bodies forbidden of freedom. And who are we,

my mother and I, these other consumers of pleasure,
to be present and not grieve this intrusion?

But this is the horror of America's song,
making a conveyor belt of oppressive systems.

In a history just before then, the land itself
might've been for sharecropping, where, for the wage

of feeding their families, people died for no income
and only leftovers before going west. When we reach

the end of our cups, as the time on our parking meter
draws to an end, we have to drive back south

to a place that has not yet been gentrified successfully
where we will sleep on the other side of town.

Self-Portrait as Unnoticed Object

You might have been anything.
        I was not expecting you there because

when I kicked you in the dark,
        that space had no name before I saw you.

Night heavy against my foot,
        I switched on the light

& there you lay,
        larger than my imagining.

You, the picture
        hung the day before, maybe two.

Dust-sized glints of light
        burst around your body

clouding the scene. You looked
        fine otherwise. Jagged shards

still stuck in the frame. Really,
        who could say you didn't find me?

If I were you,
        I would want all of me on display.

There's be no bump in the night.
        No thud. Only glass.

And blood. And bits,
        so many bits.

Dinner in Sarasota

Summer night—a tangerine sunset
over palm trees; air so densely salty,

I ask for another glass of water at our table,
and watch the condensation bubble down

the neck of my glass. Another old white person approaches
with compliments to our dining table, we

share a joke. Both compliments are similar. The first:

*What a beautiful family you have. I always wanted
a little girl like yours*—then:

*It's great you can have a meal together. Look,
not one phone out at the table; so civil!* Yes,

so peaceful. Look, how by not calling for attention, we do.
Our family seemingly worth observation, inquiry.

My cousin mentions we're the only Black people here,
asks what year I was born, and to my answer, replies

That can't be right. I ask where he was back then. He says: *Prison.*

The Sky is Mute Gray

      I.
            the rivers have grown thin
&
      there's a moon in the sky—
tonight
      that's blood like hemoglobin,
dark like
      God's children, so
say their names like they matter enough
      not to disappear,
shout
      all of their accomplishments,
strip
      every narrative that begins
violence.
      sing about them
&
      mean it with your whole chest
like
      God might spit them back
whole
      and untroubled, like how they laid in their
mother's
      arms for the first time; make our collective
screams
            a triumphant, joyous song.
Please,
      let them live.

II.
      The sky is mute grey &

the rivers have grown thin &

there's a moon in the sky &

tonight, like hemoglobin &

dark like God's children &
    their names   they matter &

enough to not disappear &

shout   their accomplishments &

strip every narrative &

that   violence &

promise that you will sing about me &

mean it with your whole chest &

God might spit them back whole

III.
     The sky is

                          thin &

tonight, like hemoglobin &

dark   children &
     their names   they matter

     every narrative
  begins   violence

promise   me &
mean it

God   spit them back whole

I Would Write But

I am growing old of this coffeeshop, all these polite spaces
to disappear & Solange's "Cranes in the Sky" is playing
while the central air is roaring like the ocean, so forgive me
I am having moment & my eyes are heavy, my throat
feels closed to shutting, & it is hardest to breathe
between thoughts—yes, I am writing to you about small deaths
& soon, I will leave this coffee shop and its cement floors;
I will be on the other side of these panes of glass when,
any moment now, my phone will alert me my Target order is ready
for me to pick up some cheaper version of Zyrtec—yes,
I am complaining about convenience, sure I am Complaining like it is a sport
because my body is tired of these polite spaces, my body knows
there are no places free of politics, knows I exist in the perception of fictions
& lies told then upheld throughout time, knows like every good story,
this, too, exists within a context, that memory is symbolic and significant,
that politically driven does not mean false, that politics are the games of some
and the means of survival for others, that, often, they are the only way to be heard.
& this might not make sense today, not with Anderson. Paak singing
this mid-summer afternoon into a lull & I might be ruining this
for the other people here who came so politely, so unworried,
to drink their coffee in peace—all these people who came, just to be.

There are Times When

My mother's love is the thing holding me together
and the thought that what might kill her son
could be her son is too much. Besides, this burning
country, filled with people who readily close their minds
before their mouths is not worthy to become a casualty for.
I want to write I have never imagined my body
overcome to the fears held inside of it, I want to write
I have not consider making myself a memory. I want to write
of my friend's old plant I've left unwatered on my windowsill,
and how I've noticed that while it doesn't bloom
it doesn't die. Instead, I'll write how my body counts
the days—sun, moon, thirst, movement, enough
never more. There are times when I love myself just enough
to think: shower, food, air, fresh laundry—
these are what I need—and there are times I become all action:
pacing, cooking, missing count of the days.
There's nowhere to go now. Nowhere on earth.
I stay inside for three days then three more, think
how easy it would be to disappear, how easy.

Undead

People pass me sight in [as] visions of silhouettes; unfamiliar bodies.
Unless I'm careful, I might only grow to see more of the undead.

Right now, I can recall two faces, my mother's and my own.
Pity it is, I know, to see wandering faces and feel only undead.

Little did I know, that death would link me to my best friend.
Escaping me know, the details, but I know they relate to our undead.

People pass my sight in visions, sometimes as memory or imagination.
Useless are my dreams where people visit, and I think they are undead.

Rightfully, I think I have a stake in the equity of my dreams, deservingly.
Plus, the resting mind shouldn't have such power, making people undead.

Like it or not, my dreams are canvases for the deceased and unforgotten.
Even when I'm all to myself, I keep thinking of spaces they are undead.

People pass my sight in strange visions, sometimes as tempered, broken light.
Usually, I end up in conversation with the visitor. I speak to the undead.

Ransoming my dreams for jewels, I'd trade what I could for simple thought.
Psychic remedy for loss, I need a new way to cope with seeing the undead.

Lodged in my bones, the warming sensation of blood is followed by violence.
Even when my thoughts are furthest from off kilter, I keep thinking of the undead.

America is in An Arms Race with Itself

And some arms stretch further than others
or were made able to, and roam freely without
detection or surveillance or another
pair of eyes glued to them and then another—
sometimes I think under the sun lies everything
darkness can't hide away, in my sincerest dreams,
I want to wish this to be true, although
I know that here all weapons do not take
the same shape or leave identical scars,
yes, sometimes they are projectiles fired
far and near, sometimes things that go boom
in the night, or they are the silences that mirror dusk,
or sometimes they are the cold eyes
that never leave you unmarked, alone.

I Think My Mother Has an Obsession with Our Last Name

I mean her home is cluttered with knick knacks displaying the name Charlton,
that she says it with a flair for the dramatic, the word leaves her lips

like she's prepared a gift for the listener, like she has access to the royalty
of the Crown, like her and the Queen of England are kinfolk,

like the Queen and her swap crowns on the weekends, you know,
when her Majesty wants to lay low for a bit and not be spotted.

She says our last name, corrections included, like, no,
not with the hard k sound, or not with an es before the t, or

my personal favorite, it sounds like the actor's name—Charlton Heston.
I think my mother's love for her last name borders on cynical.

Maybe my thoughts are too cynical, and her love is normal.
She's worn the name much longer, though, I know. She's put

more miles on the pavement of the earth walking around with that name.
I think my mother's obsession love comes from a genuine place.

She wants to hold on to it like a precious thing and had no thoughts
of giving me my father's name when I was born. This is the story

of how the name became something made for me. Really, something
made for us that we could keep together. She's said before she hates

she and her siblings all have different last names. She's said
that she hated going to school and filling out paperwork like strangers,

having to leave to the imagination where they might come from,
relying on their own stories to explain their connection.

This is one strength of a shared last name, a familiarity like a mirror,
a place to return to and see yourself in, or a place to imagine love

ever present. I mean, too, that this is a place where pride resides.
And I want to tell her this is fine. I want to tell her that the history

of the name should sound royal, that the name is British, so much so
it's Old English. First from the fifteenth century. From the ancient

Charleston, a location. A place for the people. Later used in as a name
in the seventeenth century. A signifier of people. I want to tell her

this connection to the Brits, like so many others, comes with a price.
Comes as a lasting reminder of our history as slaves. Online,

I find the record books kept from Jamaican slave trades. I see the name,
stripped of its lore and all its glory. I see the name of men, of women,

who bought, sold, and traded. These people are not my family.
These people are responsible for the legacy my family could become.

I Can't Focus Right Now, Please Call Again

I'm listening to the music of my heartbeat
pounding in my chest, a rhythm which ripples
through my body, so I lay here, alone
and naked like a corpse. I keep thinking

I am not dead yet, which is also to say
have not been killed yet. This is all luxury
and privilege, my ability to escape danger,
to distance myself from the killing machine.

I keep thinking about my last home
and its red dirt roads, tumbleweed cities;
the way highways and interstates hold the keys
to safe travels.

I know too well my privilege and wear
its gaudy glint around my neck.
This is why my head won't fit my shoulders.
Why my skin is so smooth.

I'm thinking, now, of Tulsa and the bodies
left in the street. Hundreds, thousands,
surely enough not to matter to count.
I keep thinking, keep counting
my breaths between the beats.

On Darkness

At a campsite off an Oklahoma dirt road,
we settled in the cool of the night
amidst the buzz of cicadas, the coos of owls,
the evening breeze washing over us;
you in your hammock, rocking
sometimes to adjust your reading light,
or because I nudged you with my foot.

When this close to the elms, red cedars,
the oaks, you hear them sing a new song,
a gift only heard in the silence of night.
The sound is heaven and if you're fortunate,
you'll hear it more than once in a lifetime.
But I wasn't focused on the gift
that evening. What held my attention

while I lay in the dirt—was you
saying you felt more like a white woman
than a black one. And maybe it was because
you look like your mother; that I'd never pass,
though you could, if you chose; that I'd seen
too many like me, like us, I'd thought
sent into the earth, their mothers left childless;

maybe it was the fear of my mother childless;
the sight of fathers, like yours, dark as the night,
as the feeling of grief knowing your advice for survival
had been rendered useless. Maybe that is why
I did not realize, while lying in the dirt,
that if we had only remained silent

I've Known Memory as a Portal and a Tether

There's no need for a white lie. I have no obligation to being
well-adjusted, or doing well. Now, every moment is grief, is love

for a graying memory, some small joy that breaks my heart in pieces.
What I want is the security of privilege and the ability to love

my people as we hurt. I want to learn to sing. Or maybe dance.
Not for show, but for joy, knowing that rhythm, too, is love

for the familiar; and how a cadence can give life like a heartbeat.
I want to open my lips, and instead of my voice, speak love.

To close my mouth and taste the same. Once, I cried over food.
My mother's birthday gift to me, a dish from childhood, love

for another memory. At the table, we'd become our own universe,
a galaxy of two planets and though we grew distant in orbit, love

always brings us back together. I know now, for sure
I want no more of this pain, instead, only my black mother's love.

Epistle for My Unborn Child

I watched a friend FaceTime her goddaughter
while we drank beers at the kitchen table after dinner.

They spoke like old friends. I introduced myself to the child,
told her my name and she told me hers,

returning a wide, almost toothless grin. I do not remember
her name at all, as I don't remember yours, either.

I am writing to you now because I thought of you
then as I silently cried over the shoulder

of my friend, my face out of the view of the screen.
She didn't notice at all, my friend,

because when she spoke to that little girl it seemed
like only they existed, like there was no space outside

of the one they shared, although they were states away.
I was standing in that moment, and unsure

what to do with myself, so I gathered up the empty beer bottles,
their hollow necks clinking between my fingers,

hoping not to set a bad example. I did this with a care
I do not know by name. A care I will call parental, although

I and her goddaughter are not related. I will call the care maternal
because that is the only kind of love I have known.

This is the truth, Unborn Child of mine,
I have never known a father's love

and I must share this story with you soon enough. I fear
I am incapable of the something I think I need to love you,

incapable of translating my mother's love into a language
my tongue won't know until it's ready to speak.

Slow Kill

I write to say a year ago,   I broke

and freaked out.   I write to say,

I'd hardly slept   that day or the one's

                     before without dreaming

       of my death, which seemed impending.

I write to say   it seemed simple, like an equation

             with only variable to account for: How?

Not why?   Or when?   Only the inevitable.

                 The one successful thing I had left in

                     me.
     One after another,   the reasons came.

          I'd made neat rows of my thoughts.
          I'd spent so much of my life trying to believe
          in myself.   Anything. This was different.
          Thoughts swelled in my chest and became my air.

I write to say,   then,
      I hoped against all hope
to suffocate.

Thinking if the oxygen   quit   rushing   to my brain, swelling with worry, maybe
I would make it through the day   without drowning myself,

          making the tub a final resting place.
       Or that when the question kept coming: How?
            I was thinking of my mother. &
            how'd she know?

        How would the news find her? Would she intuit

my loss? Or   would she sense my absence   with these eight states
between us?
         I'd revisit this question enough to not care.   Momentarily.
Because that's all it would take from   me.

                    Then, I thought how again she would know
         and I thought to leave a message only for her,
         although my heart would break for so many.
         I would write for her and no one else.

I'd write   she wasn't wrong to bring me into the world.
              That I'd gone into the silence I'd been searching for,
              and that it wouldn't be peaceful, only still. That in the
              days before grandfather's death,
              I mourned his absence in the silence of winter.
              That even though we'd not spoken since he left
              and fled while at grandmother's Alzheimer's

                    I cried into the breeze of every snowy day
in all the ways the body   knows before we do,
especially in passing, and   in the preparation of mine.
              Mine could have told you that things were taking a turn

for the worse but I'm no doctor.   I'm just a man
                    born into a lineage of men with a penchant for leaving.
                         This was my baptism by fire. Mine, would be the
slow
            kill of them all, the air leaving the room any moment.

I'd write that my body knows   joy and sorrow are all the same
         just sourced from different funnels in the brain. That time collapses.
         Days before my best friend's wedding,

                                          my absent father's
health turned
for the worse.   The day of the wedding, he passed.

I'll write this as the only connection I'll remember with him.
                    The joy that day prepared me for his absence.
                    I think that the joy shielded me from the thought
I had as a child that we'd be alright
some day. That we'd get it right, together. Instead, the body knows

great pains. Knows all the seasons.   I think my body knew it was the
summer solstice, a day I'd celebrated for years.   Two days before my birthday. I think

that all the days this summer
were longer than the earth's rotation around the sun,   or that the vortex that I felt
trapped in was actually the longest day of the entire year

and still the longest of my entire life,
    seemingly drawing shorter by the breath. I'd wish on every star again
        for summers in my childhood. For my mother
to pick me up from my grandmother's house.

                To be free of the hold of this summer.

I'd thought how any moment can feel like an eternity,
                and every turning of the earth
could feel   like sinking into its surface.
                I'd thought of the pool of water.
    The one thing every living creature needs, how too much of it would
    kill. The question remained:

    how? How'd they deliver the news the one thing my mother
has been trying to defend for so much of her life
couldn't make it through another day?
                Would this news become inevitable?
                Missed calls or text messages? The neighbors
                she's never met? Instead, I'm writing
                something new. Once, I called the only love
        that I've ever known maternal and this was
      true. I've never known love outside of this
    context. Instead,
    I learned my isolation was a residency in my own thoughts. Then kept
thinking, kept wondering   how. For her. Because of her.

I write this because it's a year from that moment of battling thoughts and they've
come again, unfortunately.
      I wish to write
      something different
      about   worry.

            I wish to write saying I will not kill
                        another black man
in a nation that's already so good at it.
Instead, I'll write knowing it's a slow
                        kill for any of us born into this system that
            wasn't made for us.

I Wait for a Love My Heart Needs

I think people are afraid to be honest.
But why when there's so much love in being honest?

I say people and dishonest only to seclude myself.
That's where truth should start, with each of us being honest.

What's lost in the naked truth? Is it gorgeous,
like diamonds in the light or disappointing? Be honest.

I held a lie between my teeth once until they'd rot.
There's an unbearable weight that could be lifted being honest.

This is to say it is not at all solely easy, being honest.
There are times lies get you places safer than being honest.

I know what I do because I've believed it to be true.
I don't think this makes anything factual or honest.

It seems I'm often skeptical to escape the pain of uncertainty,
the tear of anxiety that splinters my chest. Honest.

But won't you make meaning with me, out of moments?
Won't you stay long enough to hear me? Be honest.

There's little love in absence, but this is not the same
as distance. I believe this is truth, is honest.

There's a love that can find you, Jordan. It will be gentle
and cutting and strange and most important: honest.

In The Dream I Wake From

Once again, I am a child, blooming
like a snapdragon, tall and colorful
wandering my grandparent's backyard
to pick mangoes off the trees
when my grandmother hands me a metal
pole with a jerry-rigged hook at the end
that I raise into the sky looking
for red and green fruit—the kind ready
to be eaten after a warm wash under the hose.

I watch my grandmother gather mangoes
By inverting the excess length of her dress
Into a basket of sorts and her smile
Sweeps across her face, from cheek to cheek,
While the sun drapes the lazy day
In a honeydew that distracts us both.
When we realize this, we laugh together
For what feels like some kind of forever.

My grandfather places a small knife
In my hand and I pierce the skin
Of a mango and peel until its flesh
Is gold to my eyes. He sits counting pennies
At the kitchen table, rolling them in sleeves
That he'll take to the bank. He tells me
When I am finished, to join him, like before.

In the dream I wake from,
I have not seen either of them buried
Or had to drive past their vacant home
That holds my memories like I've never
Counted every speckled bit of its popcorn ceiling,

Like I haven't learned that love smells
Like a day-worn work shirt hung over a chair
Or the sound a voice makes when it calls out to you
Between the space of the floor and the tile,
Like I haven't learned that love rises to nothing
And that every delirious dream moans
With bitter music. So instead I think leave me
To me. Leave me a pink-sweet summer spinning
A boy away from every real thought
That has ever had or could be tied

Together with twine into a bouquet
Of peonies or daffodils or any small, precious
Thing that grows like a house filled with laughter
Before it, too, dies.

Last Night, While Perched in an Old Oak, A Dream

Last night, while perched in an old oak, I tightened my glance at America. As if my eyes cast this glance for the first time I could see what the gift of height favors the esteemed, the elevated. Above the crowd I watched gather, I noticed all the looks of awe and amazement. It was as if these people were celebrating, being together and watching me in my state. As my feet left the earth, I felt a new sensation in my belly that was round and hollow, like a tube or a straw. Before I could make out their faces, my head, like the beakless twin of an owl twisted all the way around, seeing the crowd gather. I could only hesitate as the light gathered in the evening and even as the people came in scores, the sound of crickets was my only undoing, the only song that comforted me. The people below danced, to the. cricket's song, I'm unsure, but there was a joy in their faces. They broke bread, like this was holy, like this was show. Last night, while perched in an old oak, I realized the metal taste that coated the inside of my mouth was blood as my feet lost their feeling, as the emptiness of my stomach ate through every part of me, that I was not like an owl or any nocturnal creature gifted with flight. I prayed to be gifted with flight, to be jolted from this terror, as I realized I was hanging from that old oak.

Summer Days Like Today

My vehicle becomes my cathedral
becomes my space of confession
where I alone find salvation.

Today, I will ride and mute the stereo,
roll all four windows to the crease
and let my thoughts run through the streets

wild and untamed. Of course,
there is no good way of saying
days like these I like to get lost

in the streets and let evening
turn to night, invite the moon
to ride shotgun through the city

and the places that string like yarn
through my memory, each road
a familiar stranger, knowing I can travel

here without navigation, better,
that I could write about the comfort
of memory, which is like fresh water,

or write to you knowing memory
is also sharper and colder than steel,
or that I've learned all the destinations

that mean anything to me: the church,
the school, my friend's apartments,
the grocery store, or how on summer days
like this one, I just want to be alone.

I Keep Forming Arguments, Sometimes with Myself

I've learned to put out every fire caused by my bitterness.
Before I could do so, I learn that my bitterness,
its wild embers, could spark a wildfire.

Worse, I learned silence could be just as destructive.
The voice internal would escape
and I'd listen to respond—punch, counterpunch,

just like any trained fighter is taught.
I was born brown in a country
that's burned bodies like mine for intimidation,

on assumption, for sport. The voice internal recognizes
these particularities, specializes in them.
I have lived with the expectation that my skin

means something more than culture. Call this prejudice
but please also call it unmitigated fear. The voice internal
worries about the unwholesome fear of others.

I worry that this language is untransmutable,
I can't often emulate the worry that sinks through me.
The voice internal fears this act of transformation.

Picture my brain like a train on a track. Picture, the locomotive
running at a consistent pace, trying to reach a destination.
Call this forward movement. There are spaces

where there are no tracks—
the locomotive has two options:
stop or derail.

I can't tell how the journey starts back up again.
Eventually, the movement keeps going and going.
That's about all I understand.

Hear Me Out

I keep drawing out these lines in my thoughts
and I can never tell when they are real
because when I least expect it, at times
they are. What am I saying? I won't open
up to any history with revisionist intentions
at heart. I know the whole is the sum of its
greatest parts and its most troubling. I
know that wind is blown into being when
low pressure systems meet high,
and I can't write to you what this means about
things we might make of opposing forces only
that the trees outside my window dance
all day and even into the night where I live,
or how when my neighbor's trash bin toppled over
last week no one stopped to gather the mess.
I could call this an act of God, but I keep thinking
how the cars would pass by when I do
and I know that is also part of the story.

It Just So Happens That Today

I feel odd and unproductive, lacking an answer to the question: to what end? I like

this question—it seems Victorian to me, something a boy playing a king might ask

the royal court, the silk-robed nobles, the disinteresting jesters; he asks, and they wait

for the clarity that timing and silence creates, like how water will keep visible almost

anything it swallows, make a reflection a newer & uncertain you, or like how

when the despondent patriarch delivers his full-bellied call, there is only silence, then

a pulse to respond, the divine need to validate, like when God rested knowing language

gave birth to what was first good, and the waves of darkness were lifted from the void.

I've felt stuck in the void, lately, and it just so happens that today it feels like home,

and this could be for any reason, really, because the trees keep burning in the west, or

because a city has thrown money at a family in exchange for a daughter. This country knows

only to throw money—sometimes to the dead and other times for them, as if a settlement

can afford you retribution. I think of a gun and the thought of my mother washes over me

then how I've never had enough faith to allow my body to float in any body of water.

The Darkest Place Under the Moon is Furthest from My Mother's Love

By which I mean her presence
as in her inviting lap for me to sit
or the stretch of her hands to secure me
by which I mean security or
the sacrifice of one's interest for another's as in
there is peace in assurance, familiarity;
idiosyncrasies that need no embodiment—
a laugh that would inspire your own, a sneeze
you'd recognize anywhere. The darkest place
where no sun can outstretch its ray
is worry, maybe grief, or anxiety,
the fear of knowing or conceiving
in the mind. What the imagination births
is as real as any structure reliant
on perception. So, when (if) I tell you
how I feel, it becomes a truth.
But to say I miss home is a parable
since home is no longer to me a place
but a person, the brightest spot of this living world,
the white of the flame. Instead,
truthfully, I am at a battle with absence,
a condition of the hear unreconcilable with the mind.

It Just So Happens that Today

I feel like a flamingo, like I'm posing one-legged, waiting to be shot on camera.
Every time I've seen a flamingo, they've been in a zoo, somewhere behind thick glass
with people staring while they hop on splotches of land try painstakingly to claim those.
Flamingos were nearly extinct in the 1800s, an invasive, non-native species to the Atlantic.

Every time I've seen a flamingo, it's been at a zoo, somewhere behind thick glass,
though, my home state wants them to be our state bird, the flamingo, but just like I told you,
flamingos were nearly extinct in the 1800s, being an invasive species taken across the Atlantic
and they'd nearly killed them all bringing them here, the flamingos, only because they could,

still, the choice now is to main stage them. They might as well entertain. I told you,
the flamingo was transplanted here, stolen for its beauty, the way it could stand on one leg.
And they'd nearly killed them all bringing them here, the flamingo, only because they could
despite being native to the Caribbean, Africa and having no ties to anywhere else, Still,

the flamingo was transplanted, stolen for its beauty, the cruel way it learned to stand on one leg
as people stared, and by force, hopped from land to land painstakingly claiming anything
that might have been native to the Caribbean, Africa and having no ties to anywhere else, now
I feel like a flamingo, like I'm posing one-legged, waiting to be shot on camera.

On the Occasion I Spent Eight Hours In the Emergency Room

I don't think I looked like a patient,
which is to say, I didn't look like the others

feverishly waiting for their number to be called,
like ticketholders anticipating the night's lottery results.

I was overdressed in my Sunday's best because
on the occasion I spent eight hours in the emergency room,

my body could choose no better day to fail me than a Sunday,
a holy day with a thorn in my flesh of Biblical proportion,

enough to make an apostle apologize,
a day of disappointment and waiting and watching children

walk around the waiting room, toys in hand,
making this claustrophobic hospital a classroom of imagination.

I wonder what they think this really is.
How their parents explain that being here

and going where they call your name might mean never returning—
there's no fear in turning into a pillar of salt there because

"to be absent from the body is to be present with the Lord," I've hear,
and on this occasion, I pray to be raptured from my failing body,

like the characters in the *Left Behind* series.
I want to leave this body here, a less-than-satisfactory sacrifice

to a lesser-god like science, like perseverance, like *Essence Magazine*.
I want to tell my mother to go home because it's Sunday,

because it's Mother's day, because it's getting late.

Monet's "Waterlilies"

After Robert Hayden

Today as the news from New York and Chicago
grips the air from out of this nation's lungs,
I teach ekphrasis of this image,
its emerald greens and cornflower blue

married in sensuous harmony, green
arms wrapped around a blue body.
They lie across the canvas, as if caught.

In small shades of cherry, the lilies—
like freckles—dot the face, or like acne,
redden the surface. Why did Monet
return to this sight so intently?

The mind's eye, like the eye of faith, itches
with an infernal discomfort. Have I written
this whole time about Monet, or you?

It Just So Happens that Today

I feel like a lion, like in the documentaries you'd see in film.
Every time I've seen a lion, I remember, the largest mane
does not indicate a skilled hunter, that the male lion, roaring
and leading the pride, sleeps while the females kill.

Out in the wild it seems simple, their killing. They kill to eat,
to sustain their lives on the meats of their prey—how gracious,
that their prey would do such a thing, don't you think? Choose
to put themselves in the way of harm, to be devoured.

One fateful verdict, and I'm thinking about the prey. Meaning
both the action of faith and the position of being, thinking,
about the words my mother sent me *pray for me, please,*
I keep on asking why God let's these things happen to black people.

I wonder how the lion learns to choose its next meal. Imagine
the evolutionary developments that made these things make sense.
Question: how does a lion not know to kill its own? Addressed:
To a Creator. Sent: from a son comforting his mother, poorly.

Sometimes I Worry

That engrossed in every story is an element of untruth,
        the unspooling of belief in some measured

polemic. Because memory privileges experience
        & favors the emboldened, those giving language

to history do so as if it were duty
        and not tyranny. I write to say there is a tingle

in the body when it knows what words
        fail to capture, that leaves a scar on so many

and presses in on you like you lie in the center of a mortar.
        Instead, my tongue turns

to plankwood, rotten and splintered at the ends.
        There are sights my eyes will never unlearn:

a copper moon floating in a cloudless night,
        the elastic light of sunshine over snowfall—

both conducting a silence holy and tender. I write knowing
        home is nowhere I can explain, nowhere

I can estimate within the map of my bones
        held together by flesh.

In all my memories, I am a child, lost
        and confused with this persisting world,

swimming against the tide to a shore
        I never remember being thrown from.

Making Sense of this New Normal

The idyllic is one of the most effective tools of tyranny.
There has never once been any golden age to return to,

no time absent of violence. In the Bible,
Cain is the father of murder. He envied his brother,

which is to say, the object of his anger also brought him joy,
brought him to an unfamiliar place no one can visit
and remain the same, as Herodotus made clear.

The earth sopped his brother's blood as Cain asked the Lord
if he were his brother's keepers. This is where we failed—

thinking we weren't made to protect one another,
that when God made us in their image, some were excluded.

Once, I marched into the shallow banks of a river
low enough to step through, journeyed upstream

found the source of the water's flow,
a crack in a mountain-tall rock, a small offering
I could fill with mud from the bank.

I had no clue what to do when I arrived with my friend,
except grab him by the shoulders, push him in,
and called this baptism.

I think I'm Becoming a Regular to this Neighborhood

On most days, I find myself on these streets running,
although if I am being honest, I find myself walking
my way through this sweltering heat.

Ninety degrees is the song this week of summer sings
until one hundred will peak its head through the clouds.
Today, I am not fearful for my life. Today,

I return down this street as a cyclist. I ride
Kennedy Ave. on an old bike from a friend
moving to a place halfway across the country.

These streets are safe and quiet, which is also to say,
white and unassuming, which is also to say,
here, on Kennedy Ave. I stand out, am a visitor. Today,

I am not fearful for my life, although, halfway
through this neighborhood, my body wonders,
then worries. Across the country, my mother worries.

In the distance, as I see while I rest against my bike,
children throw pebbles into the sky,
trying to knock a wasp's nest from the gutter

of their house—white painted stucco, a Gable roof.
Below the lip of the hill, a basement window visible
from this side of the street.

I watch, in some unfamiliar horror.
Their stones reach for the sky
then descend to the ground.

I'm Thinking of a Distant Future

> *Life is, in itself and forever, shipwreck.*
> —José Ortega y Gasset

And how on the first day,
black lay bare, uninhibited

over the unassuming face
of the earth in its youth

& it was beautiful.
It might take lifetimes

to tumble in that dark
again, like how planets

in foreign solar systems
dance to unfamiliar suns.

I believe our story is familiar
how we've made home of stardust

and space waste, how we survive
shipwrecked on this shore of tragedy.

8:46

The leaves have grown green
unlike you remembered. Spring
came and passed so soon.

From the living room
you watch the summer rainfall
and still remain dry.

These days seem so long
and summer light sparkles warm
over a flat land.

You could watch the moon
every day this summer
and think about death.

You pray for days short
and uneventful in May
almost every year.

For hours you watch
a screen while the summer day
comes and goes so fast.

Ninety-five degree
summer day. You hear some birds
make song all day long.

At this point, the heat
now seems less important than
say the cost of life.

To write, this summer,
is to see the dead appear
in every pen jot.

A plague cleared the streets
then a man played God, holding
down a mother's child.
 You want to return
to the summer before now
and forget this one.

Some quiet is good,
some quiet is tear gas
splitting the June sky.

You've made plans and plans
all summer but still forget
almost all of them.

Where There Is No Law

There is no need for cellphone video

        or   the commentaries, the disregard

        or   identity politics, three officers of color

        or   an autopsy, that word again: fentanyl

        or   a charge like an afterthought, third degree

        or   cities burning in the night, unholy light

        or   boarded up windows, teargas, Lincoln, Nebraska

        or   a curfew, a state of emergency, Omaha, Nebraska

        or   a bar owner, a scuffle, James' name in headlines

        or   the need to be untraceable in the crowds, airplane mode

        or   cartons of milk missing from the grocer, tear gas remedies

        or   unmarked vans lining the street, the national guard

        or   maybe, the national guard, maybe

        or   all those speeches, all that language wasting away

        or   a desire to get back to normal

        or   all the missed days, the memories we'd given away

        or   wounds, untreatable, most below the surface

        or   what seems most sensible, unimaginable before

There is no need for a knee on a person's neck

That's Not Who I Am

Even when my actions are mine,
they are not me, when I am white.
When I am white, I am always a man
and always right, as in correct. White
for so long meaning absolute, or solely observable.
In every room when I am my whitest
every person accepts me, looks me in the eyes,
tells me how well I speak, how my words
paint pictures like Picasso, like Monet, only
less Spanish, less French. Really, more like
Rockwell—oh how he painted so vividly
and imaginatively with broad strokes of freedom,
of simple life! The polite and unpolitical.
Like The Last Ear of Corn where a little boy,
his grandfather enjoy ears of corn at a table.
Simple virtues: eating at the table. When I am white,
I always make sure to say grace. Sometimes twice
thankful that, at my whitest, I am not me
even when my actions are.

Intro

I mean to write
these poems
smell of sunshine
and sweat, dead skin
wafting over the surface
of this, my one body,

and the soft absence
keeping isolation
painting the walls
of all my insides new:
the apartment, my skull,
my aching belly,
the paling whites
on the insides of my hands,

hands that made this grief
like cake, small and sweet,
though really, I mean to write,
about how I love introductions

and first impressions.
All the above, you see,
are parts of my obsession,
and I wish I could write
a different, more meaningful
conclusion saying this
obsession, my mind's
constant and embalming
making and remaking
of the things I know
and learn
were not my motivation to live.

And what I might write,
if bold enough, is how
many of my favorite
albums begin with intro:
and in this way, tell me
what I need to know
before I get into the action.

Because what I would write,
if bold enough, is how
often, I resisted my feelings
yes, because of everything
I have been taught about being a man,
and, yes, about everything
I have been taught about being black,
and yes, too, about the truth
of how being both can be so difficult
and beautiful, which really

is to say we begin here:
I struggled worse than ever
with the idea of suicide
two days before my birthday,
by which I mean to write
a new story. I mean,
I write to start again.

Notes & Additional Acknowledgments

My gratitude is much larger than my ability to list and name. *Slow Kill* exists as a gift of so many people's time, energy, shared grace, and encouragement. My first thank you goes to my mother for her unflinching and unwavering belief in me. I would call her by name, but she'd probably think that was strange or out of line. In the off chance that, by reading this collection of poems, she's developed a softer side, here goes nothing: I love you, and I am thankful for you, Tanya Charlton.

I am grateful to the editors and readers of the following publications where many of these poems were first shared with the world, such as *Platform Review, Rappahannock Review, West Trade Review, Ruminate, Atticus Review, Brushfire: A Literary & Arts Journal, Lucky Jefferson, Mount Island, Typehouse Literary Magazine, Shift: A Journal of Literary Oddities*, and *The Journal*.

So much of my appreciation goes to Leah Huete de Maines and the team at Finishing Line Press. I'm grateful for you all, and for the faith you have in this work. Thank you for publishing my debut—the only one I'll get! Similarly, I'm so thankful for my professors and mentors like Grace Bauer, Ted Kooser, Joy Castro, Kwame Dawes, Amelia Montes, Julia Schleck, Hope Wabuke, and Stacey Waite. So many of these poems were inspired by the encouraging words of Kwakiutl Dreher—thank you.

Isaiah Jones, thank you, for this dream of a cover and the willingness to work with me on it.

Likewise, thank you to my Lincoln family: Jamaica Baldwin, Saddiq Dzukogi, Angel Garcia, Kate Gaskin, David Henson, Claire Jimenez, Erika Lukert, Jess Poli, Katie Schmid, Alina Nguyen, Olufunke Ogundimu, Alex Ramirez, Ava Winter, and others for teaching me what it means to be a member of a supportive writing community and for helping me believe in my own voice.

Gina Tranisi—yours is a voice I always trust. Riley Westerholt, I'm so thankful for you; love you; grateful to share a brain with you. Derrick Funk, Tina Le, Antonio Hamersky, Francesca Rorhs, and the lively bunch at Lincoln East High School, thank you for years of the greatest joy I had while writing. Isaac Essex, Syble Heffernan, Em Hammans Celie Knudsen, Caitlin Matheis, Elva Moreno, Caleb Peterson, thank you, friends, for all the lessons and laughs along this writing life.

Thank you, Oklahoma. Thank you, Trey Moody, for always being a committed teacher, mentor, and friend. Thank you for giving me the confidence to write.

For the incarcerated writers I've had the privilege to work with, I wish you all the best; I'm thankful for all that we were able to learn together.

Maya Pierce, you are one of my favorite artists and greatest friends. Ale Sanchez, my love to you. Zamira Atluhanova, my mini-me, thank you, love you, we'll travel somewhere fun soon.

Josh Cox, Avery Evans, Seth Liggins, Dontá Love, Braden Stuart, Keygan, and Zac Helms, you all mean the world to me. You've believed in me before I did, and still do.

My gratitude is with you all forever.

Jordan Charlton is a poet and Ph.D. student at the University of Nebraska-Lincoln. His work has appeared in *The Adroit Journal, Quarter After Eight, Ruminate, The Journal,* and elsewhere. In his work with The Nebraska Writer's Collective, he's facilitated workshops with both high school poets and incarcerated writers through the programs All Writes Reserved and Writers' Block.

www.ingramcontent.com/pod-product-compliance
Lightning Source LLC
Chambersburg PA
CBHW020342170426
43200CB00006B/479